Every Day Isn't Perfect

Volume I: Change Begins With You First

D1315867

by Dr. K. L. Register

Every Day Isn't Perfect

Original and modified cover art by NaCDS and CoverDesignStudio.com

First Edition: June 2016

Printed in The United States of America.

ISBN-13: 978-1533398550

ISBN-10: 1533398550

Scriptures are taken from King James Version. Public Domain.

"For God hath not given us the spirit of fear; but of power, and of love, and of a sound mind." (2 Timothy 1:7)

Dedication

This book is dedicated to

the person who has been afraid

to muster up the ***courage***

needed to take a chance.

Today is your lucky day.

Just keep reading …

Contents

Contents

Contents

Contents

Introduction

"*A strong woman knows that greatness can be achieved when she focuses on lifting others up instead of tearing them down.*"

Welcome to Volume I of the journey of a fun – loving farm girl, chemist, and dentist who hates the taste of macaroni and cheese, but loves the taste of spaghetti. Born and raised on a farm in the rural parts of South Georgia, my life has been a continuous voyage of self – discovery. After twenty – three years and a bachelor's degree, I had a few hesitations about trading in my cowgirl boots for scrubs in the charming town of Augusta. But after four years of dental school, I eagerly handed in my scrubs for high heels in the big city of Atlanta. Although the big city was quite entertaining, I decided to let go of my heels for swimsuits on the beaches of Savannah. Savannah – the beautiful and peaceful place I call home. Well, at least it has been home for the past seven years. Only God knows where I might be or what I may trade my swimsuits in for in a few more years …

Over the past seventeen months, my mind and body have eagerly anticipated the birth of my little bundle of joy – **this book**. Based upon my own unique personal experiences as well as the thought – provoking experiences of others, the content of this book was written with the same love and attention to detail that a mother would give to her newborn. It was written first and foremost with **you** in mind: to help you discover who you really are, encourage you to love and believe in yourself, challenge you to become your very best self, and inspire you to follow your dreams.

As you read, you will discover …

This book is a collection: a mixture of short stories and prose telling the stories of human hopes and fears. Each story and prose has an original quote below its title. Embodied within every set of quotation marks is a positive message that will enhance your life. As you read, dig deep within yourself to uncover the answers to helpful questions such as:

Who am I?

What is my purpose in life?

Am I living my dreams?

Who/What is most important to me?

What do I want out of life?

What do I need to make me happy?

Where am I headed? How do I get there?

Your answers to these questions are important and will give your life a sense of direction.

As you read, you will discover ...

Although this book is not lengthy in pages, it is varied and filled with substance. Within five chapters, you will find out what happens when you: believe that your life has a special purpose, change the way you view yourself, your life, as well as the world, open your heart and mind up to new possibilities, learn to maneuver around life's unpredictable obstacles, hold on to and let go of the right people, and embrace the spirits of hope and positivity. Within five chapters, you will experience my life as well as the lives of others, the meaningful good, the painful bad, and the unpleasant ugly, as if you were present in the moment. This will be a personal and intimate journey of self – exploration and self – discovery; a journey of acceptance, courage, gratitude, forgiveness, hope, happiness, and love.

But remember, not just my journey: *your* journey as well.

Now sit back and relax, grab some popcorn and a blanket, and let's begin our journey. Keep in mind as you read, although every day of your life has a purpose, *"Every Day Isn't Perfect."*

Chapter 1:

Faith and Purpose

Who's Searching For Me?

"The color you paint on your lips doesn't make you any more beautiful, but the color you paint on the world with your heart does. What color are you painting?"

I used to be hesitant to show people who I really was, because I was worried that they would judge the woman on the inside just as harshly as they had judged the woman on the outside. Every time I closed my brown eyes, I would hear multiple voices echoing within my head, "She is too skinny, she is too fat, she is too tall, she is too …"

I allowed their perception of me to influence me. Their voices became my voice. Their words became my words. Their thoughts became my thoughts. Their beliefs became my beliefs. Their lies became my truth.

Many days were spent trying to be seen as the "perfect" woman in their eyes: the over – ambitious, God – fearing woman who always had her "picture perfect" life together. My soul craved and thirsted for their physical attention and verbal approval as bad as a newborn baby desired the sweet delicious taste of her mother's breast milk. I wanted people to like me, love me, value me, and appreciate me. My self – esteem needed to feel validated at all times. The more I aimed to please other people, the more I hid who I really was. The more I hid who I was, the more depressed my soul became.

It was only a matter of time before I no longer knew who I was. My physical and spiritual identities had faded away just as quickly as sand fades from in between a child's stubby fingers at the beach on a windy day. I kept searching for someone and something within other people, not realizing the someone I was searching for was me and the something I was longing for was God's purpose for me.

After years of experiencing life: the joys and heartaches ... the ups and downs ... I finally found the woman I was searching for. And I also found the purpose I was longing for. Unfortunately, it took me quite a while to see that just as hard as I was searching for her and God, she and God were also searching just as hard for me.

The Pieces of My Puzzle

"A smile doesn't mean everything in your life is perfect. It just means you are thankful for the imperfect life you have."

I opened up my rugged cardboard box

Within lay the years of my imperfect life

Randomly mixed up and assorted

Jig – sawed into a thousand individual pieces

Hand painted and intensely colored

Irregular in shape and uneven in size

Curved, crooked, and straight edges

Interlocked …

Precious and painful memories

Intertwined …

Piece by piece my puzzle revealed

A complete picture of my perfectly imperfect life

Whoa! How Did I Get Here?

"Sometimes, you are guided down a different pathway than you originally had planned. Trust your intuition; it will let you know if you are on the right path."

There have been moments in my life in which I have questioned whether or not there was a God, a Heaven, and a Hell. Although many people have asked themselves similar questions, most Christians would not dare admit to anyone that they have questioned their own religious beliefs. We (Christians) desire to be seen as the one who has the strongest mustard seed faith, the one with the closest relationship with the Creator, or the one who understands the symbolic messages of the Bible better than anyone else on this Earth.

Over the years, quiet moments of self – reflection have given my mind the permission to be human and to connect the pieces of my puzzle. After experiencing personal life events as I have, such as the sudden closing of one door and the immediate opening of another and the appearance of opportunities completely out of the blue (beyond my control) I began to:

1. realize that I did not arrive at where I am today all on my own.
2. develop a personal (spiritual) relationship with God.
3. have faith (trust) that God's spirit lives within me.
4. accept that there is a purpose for my life: I'm here for a reason.
5. believe that everything happens for a reason.
6. show gratitude for the blessings and opportunities given to me.
7. pray for guidance as well as for the desires of my heart.
8. seek and depend on God during times of need or distress.
9. ask for forgiveness.
10. respect that each individual has his/her own personal beliefs.

What If There Was No Heaven?

"Your personal beliefs are your personal beliefs. You don't owe anyone any type of scientific explanation or physical proof."

What if there was no heaven
What would happen to our souls
Would our physical bodies evaporate into this ole' earth
mute lips, blind eyes, and deaf ears

Silenced

Physically and spiritually paralyzed
within a pitch black coma
permanently unable to breathe or move

What if there was no heaven
Would we be translated to a foreign earth
a world that unknowingly exists beyond our
visible moon, stars, and sun

And if we were to be translated
Would we still be the same person
who we are today
would our long lost loved ones be there with us
or would we be born to merely die once again

What if there was no heaven
Would we simply turn to insignificant dust
my mind has allowed me to wonder
but, my soul in God
I will forever entrust

Spirit Of Fear

"If you aren't expecting great things to happen in your life, your expectations are too low. Expect great things!"

For years I'd been too afraid to enjoy some of the happiest moments of my life, always expecting things to go wrong. I could quote the Bible verse [1]"God hath not given us the spirit of fear" with my eyes closed while turning a cartwheel. But still a lingering voice kept repeating over and over again, "You are not worthy."

After many years of thinking negatively, doubting myself, procrastinating, fearing rejection, fearing the unknown, over – analyzing situations, stressing about problems, and complaining about life not being fair, I began to listen and read. And knowledge gave me the burning desire to change my way of thinking (attitude) from negative to positive. By reading inspirational literature, such as the Bible and self – help books and blogs, meditating on the advice of my mother and mentors, listening to the testimonies and life stories of those who have endured hardship and overcame, and reflecting upon the life lessons I have learned from past experiences, I'm learning to appreciate the good that comes my way.

No, I am not perfect. I still have my days where the journey seems scary. But now when fear attempts to linger, I have learned to recognize its presence: what it feels, looks, and sounds like. And I make every effort to shift my thoughts to let fear know that I recognize its presence and will not allow it to succeed. As each brand new day begins, I remind myself, "You only get one life. And life comes with both happiness and sadness. Why not spend most of your time enjoying it?"

Now close your eyes, smile, and enjoy. Because just like me, *you* are worthy as well!

The Internal Power

"The internal power needed to maneuver around any obstacle is within you. Ignite your power with belief in yourself!"

When I was a teenager, I was once told by a prophet that it was not in God's will for me to become a dentist. And for years after being told that, I was scared to pursue my dream. As I continued through two more years of high school as well as three years of college, the idea of becoming a dentist had become a distant memory.

Nevertheless, God gave me the strength, courage, wisdom, and faith (internal power) needed to achieve my lifelong dream. A dream that I love shared with patients, staff, friends, and family that I love. Everyday isn't perfect. And the journey hasn't always seemed perfect. But what God has in His will, is and will forever be perfect.

My heartfelt message is simple:

Just because you accomplish one dream, two dreams, or a thousand dreams doesn't mean you stop dreaming. Never stop believing in your dreams!

Pause for a moment. Write down one dream that you would love to accomplish. Refer back to this page as often as you need. It should serve as a reminder of what you can and will accomplish.

Dream:

_____

_____

Never In My Plans

"There will be times when you will fight against God's plan because you are unsure of what's happening. But trust that He is molding you to do your work!"

I graduated from college within three years with almost a 4.0 GPA in Chemistry, and I worked at a call center for a few months after graduation. Always the shy and quiet person, working at a call center was never in my plans. I was too embarrassed to tell my close family and friends that I even worked there. In their eyes, I was supposed to be living the life of a successful and rich mad scientist.

But in reality, I didn't have much of a choice. I couldn't find a job in my field, and I desperately needed the money. Little did I know, God was preparing me to do what I now love. He was teaching me how to communicate (*my purpose*): to talk, listen, laugh, cry, and share my heart with people. He was also laying the foundation that now allows me to successfully provide for my patients.

Now keep in mind, working at a calling center was never in my plans. But surely it was in God's plans, and that is what has made the greatest difference.

My heartfelt message is simple:

In order to discover who you truly are and what you are really made of, you will have to go through some things. Just because you don't understand what you are going through or why you are going through it does not mean that there isn't a reason behind you going through it. Whether you fully understand it or not, keep moving forward with confidence and faith! Trust and believe that all things are working in your favor.

Silent Whispers Of A Hopeful Man

"It's difficult for hope and doubt to dwell in the same place.
Release the spirit of doubt in order to embrace the spirit of hope."

We live,
We live in a world
in which sometimes it seems
as if our prayers, sorrows, or dreams
go unanswered

causing us
to question
in our spiritual minds
whether God
whether our God
Does our God truly exist

We live,
We live in a world
in which sometimes it seems
as if our fathers, brothers, or friends
turn their backs on us

causing us
to wonder
in our emotional hearts
whether love
whether true love
Does true love really exist

We live,
We live in a world

in which sometimes it seems as if
our decisions, choices, or mistakes
blind us from seeing the vision

causing us
to doubt
in our physical minds
whether victory
whether our victory
Does our victory actually exist

We live,
We live in a world
in which sometimes it seems as if
we just don't understand

But **Hope** …
hope in a living God
hope in sweet love
hope in good people
hope in a united nation
hope in a better tomorrow

gives us the
courage to fight
strength to believe and,
reason to never ever
give up

What's Your Shoe Size?

"The tears, the mistakes, the disappointments, and the heartaches are all part of life's battle. Keep fighting!"

One night while in Bible study, a prophet called me to the front of the church and asked, "What do you want to be after you finish high school?"

My response was, "I want to be a dentist."

And his response was, "But that is not what God wants you to be." After hearing his message, I left church that night with my Bible in one hand and pieces of my heart in the other.

One afternoon while at a friend's house, her mother asked, "What are you going to do after you finish college?"

I said, "I'm not sure. I want to be a dentist. But I'm scared."

Her response was, "Why would you want to do that? You should go to medical school. You're way too smart to be a dentist." After hearing her message, I left my friend's house with my textbook in one hand and pieces of my heart in the other.

Lastly, one night while at home, my dad asked, "What are you going to do now since you've turned down a good job with The Bureau? Just because you say you want to be some dentist." After hearing his message, I just cried.

All three of these moments were disappointing to me. But the very last moment made me realize it was now time for me to pursue my dream! It was now time for me to begin my work!

My Heartfelt Message:

The footprint you leave on this world is the work you do while you are here. It starts with you and a simple prayer, a humble belief, an inspirational hope, a tireless dream, a captivating idea, a strong purpose, a courageous mission, or a heartfelt passion.

But no one said that the journey would be easy.

Sometimes in order to achieve your goals, you have to let go of the opinions and beliefs of others surrounding you. You have to let go of the idea that just because others think it, believe it, or speak it: it will be so. There will be times when you have to make a way, even when no one else in this world believes there is a way. There will be times in which you have to boldly look fear dead in the face and let it know that you are more than a conqueror. And there will be times when you will doubt yourself, doubt God, and doubt the whole journey. And life will make you wonder, "Did I make the right choice?"

But I live to tell you:

Every triumph, every defeat, every mastery, and every mistake allows you to become a stronger person, a wiser person, and a better person. A unique lesson can be learned from all of life's experiences. Sometimes, you don't realize the lesson until you start to put some of the pieces of your puzzle (past experiences) together. This collection of past experiences is also what teaches you how to trust yourself; have faith that your decisions and choices will guide you one step closer to fulfilling the desires that repeatedly ache within you (***your purpose and your dreams***).

I will leave you with this:

You don't have to be perfect to achieve your dreams. You don't even have to have all of the details of the game plan figured out. The only thing you have to do is simply be willing to do your work!

Do Dreams Really Come True?

"Your personal success has to be your priority, responsibility, and story. You have to make a conscious choice to want more, do better, and become greater."

After graduating from dental school, I moved to Atlanta with dreams of making the big city my home. But there was only one small problem: I was a new graduate with no guidance, no experience, and no confidence. For months, I whined and complained to my mother over the phone, via text, and in person. Boy, was I mad at the whole doggone world. I couldn't believe I had gone to school for seven years, accumulated an enormous amount of student loan debt, and still could not find the job of my dreams. A part of me had begun to think, "Maybe, that prophet was right."

One morning, I decided to visit a dental job consultant for a bit of helpful advice. After instructing me to have a seat, the consultant asked me several questions. One of the questions he asked was, "What type of dental office are you looking for?"

My response was, "I'm looking for a mentor, a family, and a place where I can grow."

He smiled and said, "You sure are looking for a lot. Do you know how many dentist dream of that? Good luck!"

After leaving the consultant's office, I returned to my apartment drenched with tears of discouragement. Gloom gently held my hand as I blindly staggered through the front door. I laid down on the sofa. My mind began to wander into a sea of pitch black darkness. Suddenly, I remembered glancing at an email that was sent by a classmate. The three – month – old email had read, "Dr. Martin is looking for an associate general dentist in the Savannah area." Although I had never imagined living in Savannah, I figured I had nothing to lose by giving this Dr. Martin fellow a call.

The next day, I called Dr. Martin. Little did I know that one phone conversation would change my life forever. Dr. Martin kindly invited me to his dental office for a job interview.

A couple of days following my interview, Dr. Martin called and offered me the associate general dentist position at his office. But there was only one small problem: I still didn't have any experience or confidence. Nevertheless, I now had a mentor and guidance. With my guidance there came experience; with my experience there came confidence.

Many times, I have wished that I could call that dental consultant and let him know what I have found: God gave me a mentor, a family, and a place where I could grow. He surrounded me with a team who prays together, laughs together, cries together, and works together to deliver the best dentistry that a dental office can give.

A team whose flesh has been formed by the hands of Dr. Martin and Mrs. Martin, whose backbone has been strengthened by the dedication of our team, and whose heart beats through the smiles of each and every one of our patients. Wow! What I'd give to let that consultant know ... that dreams really do come true!

When Broken Stones Cried

"Your life story is written every day. But it isn't written with ink. It's written with purpose. You are here for a reason!"

Innocent rocks wept
At the garden's gate
Broken stones cried
Tears of red clay
Rocks scattered swiftly
With the northwest winds
Pieces gathered purposefully
By my Father's hands
Molded clay smiled
A man was formed
In one breath
Rocks were given a soul

Innocent rocks wept
At the garden's gate
Broken man cried
Tears of clear pain
Life wandered lonely
With the southwest winds
Man gathered purposefully
By my Father's hands
Molded rib loved
A woman was formed
In two breaths
Rocks were given a soul

Innocent rocks wept
At the garden's gate
Broken man cried
Tears of guilt and shame
Woman digressed sinfully
With the northeast winds
Sinners gathered purposefully
By my Father's hands
Molded spirit lived
The Christ was formed
In one breath
Rocks were given a soul

Innocent rocks wept
At the garden's gate
Broken sinners cried
Tears of God's pain
Life repented genuinely
With the southeast winds
Christ gathered purposefully
By my Father's hands
Molded spirit died
So that *you* could be formed
In two breaths
Rocks were given a soul

Chapter 2:

Philosophy and Wisdom

Be Careful Who You Listen To

"If you seek approval from the outside, you won't ever be good enough. If you seek approval from the inside, who you are becomes good enough."

Dear Self,

People will say you are not pretty enough, wise enough, strong enough, or good enough; so many people will freely cast doubt on your self – esteem

Countless numbers of voices whispering into your ears; speaking with confidence out of both sides of their mouths

As if they know who you are, what you want, what you need, or what will work best for you; better than you will ever know for yourself

As if God did not make you in His image. Beautiful enough to attract the soul of the king who will love you for you: natural beauty, raw flaws, subtle imperfections, vulnerable emotions, and human fears

As if you are not capable of accomplishing the desires of your heart; a heart committed to working together with your mind to intellectually and wholeheartedly discover where the running rivers of life need your spirit to flow

As if the fibers of your being were not equipped by God to weave through the unexpected trials and unforeseen burdens that the running rivers will throw your way

As if the sore bruises on the bottom of your feet and the coarse calluses on the underside of your hands will make you unable to walk, run, swim, or handle the course that God has anointed with His purpose

As if God did not make *you* alone … enough

Be careful who you listen to
People will attempt to poison your spirit
With harmful words that are absorbed by your ears

Yep! They Said It!

"Self – acceptance begins the second you grant yourself the permission to love who you are: inside and out."

Eight years ago, someone said, "Push away from the table."

Seven months ago, someone said, "You are too skinny."

Six minutes ago, I said, "I am who I am."

Maybe She Needs To Push
Away From The Table

"You will miss out on what life is calling you to do if you're tuning into the wrong channels. Pray. Meditate. Listen. Prepare. Fight. Win. Victory is yours!"

The first day I walked through the double doors of dental school, I weighed 120 lbs. The last day I walked through those same doors, I weighed 160 lbs. Over the course of four years, I had gained 40 lbs. Never did I imagine that French fries, ice cream, milkshakes, and stress (The Unhealthy Four) would become my closest colleagues. We had studied anatomy together. We had treated patients together. And we dreamed of one day practicing dentistry together.

In our fairy – tale, we would spend the rest of our lives together.

After graduation, my relationship with The Unhealthy Four continued to develop. We moved to Atlanta with the hopes of meeting new people, but I was the only one who didn't want to mingle. We moved into a new apartment with dreams of exploring the big city, but I was the only one who didn't want to go anywhere. We had bought new clothes with the intentions of wearing them like supermodels on the runway in Paris.

But who was I kidding? I couldn't bear to look at my reflection in the mirror. Deep down on the inside, I was ashamed of the woman I saw on the outside.

As my relationship with The Unhealthy Four became more intimate, people wanted to know the answer to a particular question:

"Are you pregnant?" they asked.

"No, I'm not pregnant!" I answered.

"Good for you! Well, maybe you need to push away from the table" they advised.

My inner spirit felt sadder than a kitten who couldn't find her way back home. I had allowed my own negative thoughts as well as the negative opinions of others to smother my joy, strangle my passion, and suffocate the zeal I once had for life.

One evening while lying in my bed, an unfamiliar voice whispered the words, "Now isn't the time to give up! Get up!"

I sat straight up in my bed.

Was this the voice of an angel? Was this the voice of God? Or, was this my own voice? I wasn't sure of whose voice I had heard. However, there was one thing I knew for certain.

This was a sign! It was time for ***change***!

My focus became learning how to live and maintain a healthy life. Over the next month or so, I read every health blog published in the year 2008. I also created a written list of physical goals that I wanted to achieve. In order for my plan to be a success, I knew I had to be honest with myself. It was important for me to set realistic goals.

Woo Hoo! Over the course of seven months, I lost 40 lbs. I was amazed at how well my plan had worked. Over the next seven years, I have maintained my body weight at 125 lbs – 130 lbs. Currently, I weigh 125 lbs. As my relationship with The Unhealthy Four became more distant, people wanted to know the answer to another question:

"How do you stay so slim?" they asked.

"Here are the secrets that helped me" I answered.

Secret 1: Kick stress to the curb!

Just like you, I spent many sleepless nights worrying about my body image, crying over relationships, stressing about my career, struggling with money, and questioning my religion. Over time, I learned to accept that we all have our daily burdens to bear and challenges to overcome.

Psst! Here are some words of wisdom: There isn't a challenge on this planet that you will face that someone else has not been through and overcame. It's not the actual challenge that breaks you down, but how you choose to respond to the challenge that makes the difference.

If overcoming an unhealthy lifestyle was my heart's desire, it was time for me to ask myself, "Are you going to wallow in a muddy pit of stress and self – pity or are you going to put your size 10.5 boots on and climb your way out of this mess?"

Personal Recommendation: Grab your boots! Put both feet in! And remind yourself, "Life could always be worse!"

Secret 2: Allow yourself to accept you!

After visiting health and fitness blogs and reading beauty and fashion magazines, I realized that the ancient gods were absolutely right: What may seem unattractive to one person may appear amazingly beautiful to someone else.

It was totally okay for me to not have the body of Heidi Klum, Tyra Banks, or Jennifer Lopez. My goal was no longer to look like a supermodel on the runway in Paris. My goals were to be healthy, look healthy, and feel good about who I was (on the inside and out). Now, don't get me wrong. If my body looked like that of Klum, Banks, or Lopez as a result of working hard to achieve my goals, I wasn't going to complain.

Personal Recommendation: Ten minutes of reading, writing, meditation, or self – reflection in a quiet place every day.

Secret 3: Make wiser choices!

After making my decision to follow my heart, I constantly had to remind myself, "You have to give yourself time." I wanted change to happen overnight, but unfortunately life doesn't always work that way. One has to give him/herself time to adjust to such a drastic lifestyle change. During my transition period, I made a conscious effort to make smarter food and drink choices. This process involved being mindful of when I was eating, the types of food I was eating, and how much I was eating.

Slowing down and thinking about the consequences of putting a fistful of potato chips in my mouth or two pieces of key lime cake on my plate became essential. Making a grocery list prior to grocery shopping felt like overkill, but it helped. Carefully reading over the menu at a restaurant in order to make healthier substitutions seemed tiresome at first, but later became easier: steamed broccoli instead of French fries, balsamic dressing instead of ranch dressing, water instead of lemonade.

Personal Recommendation: Think about the consequences of your actions before you react!

Secret 4: Don't forget to treat yourself!

Prior to going grocery shopping each week, I would research (online and in magazines) and make out a list of foods that I wanted to try but hadn't ever thought about buying. This new way of grocery shopping allowed me to discover a variety of healthy foods that tasted pretty good: zucchini, asparagus, spinach, broccoli, cauliflower, red onions, and walnuts. But I didn't go cold turkey and give up all of the foods I loved.

Question: So what had changed?

Answer: I taught myself how to eat the unhealthy foods in smaller proportions and less frequently than the healthier foods. I learned to be mindful of when I was eating, the types of food I was eating, and how much I was eating.

Personal Recommendation: Find a good balance between the healthy and unhealthy foods!

Secret 5: Don't skip meals!

Before embarking on my new journey, I used to skip meals in hopes of losing weight faster. But I quickly found out that skipping meals caused more harm than good. Not only did it make me feel irritable and weak, but skipping meals also made me feel extremely hungry causing me to overeat at my next meal. Overtime, I found breakfast to be the most critical meal of the day. It provided my brain and body with the initial boost of energy needed to effectively master my hectic day.

My Personal Regimen:
Breakfast: Fruit, Meat, Yogurt
Lunch: Healthy Frozen Dinner, Raw Vegetables, Snack
Dinner: Meat, Cooked Vegetables, Starch

Personal Recommendation: Eat three large meals or multiple small meals throughout the day. Experiment and find out what works best for you!

Secret 6: Discipline your body!

Although, my life had its fair share of unpredictable moments, my body functioned best when a daily routine was followed. After a couple of weeks, eating three meals around the same time every day became a regular part of my schedule.

My schedule:
Breakfast: 8:30 am – 9:00 am
Lunch: 1:00 pm – 2:00 pm
Dinner: 5:30 pm – 7:30 pm

I usually avoid eating anything after 7:30 pm. If I must have something else to eat after 7:30 pm, I have found fresh fruit and/or raw vegetables to be enjoyable snacks.

Personal Recommendation: Make a schedule! And stick to it!

Secret 7: Eat your fruits and vegetables!

I used to have really embarrassing acne that left my skin severely hyper – pigmented and uneven in tone. After I began eating more fruits and vegetables, I gradually noticed a difference in my skin tone. It felt smoother, it looked more even, and it screamed **radiant**!

My friends asked the question, "Girl, who's making you **glow**?"

Little did they know, "His name was Beta – Carotene!"

Personal Recommendation: Eat at least one serving of fruit at breakfast, two servings of vegetables at lunch, and two servings of vegetables at dinner!

Secret 8: Drink plenty of H₂O!

I drank more water throughout the day when I purchased a portable water container. The reason my daily intake increased was because the container was more convenient, allowed me to be more disciplined, and gave me more flexibility. It could easily be taken to the gym, mall, office, movies, or football games.

The current recommended daily intake of water is one – half of one's body weight in ounces (oz). Since I weigh between 120 lbs – 130 lbs, my recommended intake is approximately 60 oz of water per day.

My Schedule:
20 oz of water with breakfast
20 oz of water with lunch
20 oz of water with dinner

Personal Recommendation: Drink at least one – half of your body weight in oz of water every day!

Secret 9: Get up and move!

The first week of starting a new exercise regimen had always been the most difficult for me. I found myself attempting to work out like I was LeBron James' sister. However, there were always two small problems: I wasn't LeBron James' sister, and I was out of shape. I would feel great the first two to three days after beginning a routine. But once that lactic acid built up in my thighs and calves, the game was over before it had fully begun. Days four and five were officially quitting time!

After months of experimentation, I discovered plenty of activities that I could do to burn calories throughout my day: Walk! Run! Jumping jacks! Cut the grass! Squats in front of the TV! Sit – ups to my favorite songs! Dance while cleaning the house! Take the stairs! Go to the gym! The most important part was getting my heart rate UP!

Personal Recommendation: Do at least thirty minutes of physical activity four to five days per week!

Secret 10: Get your beauty rest!

Prior to making a commitment to living a healthy life, I had no idea how important sleep was to my overall health. I had spent seven years in college and dental school (combined) working on projects, writing research papers, and cramming for exams all night long. Talking on the phone, roaming the internet, and watching TV until the wee hours of the morning was considered normal to me.

Over the years, I had to train myself to go to bed by a certain hour. Everything is turned off when the large hand strikes 11:00 pm: this includes TV, computer, cell phone, and lights.

Personal Recommendation: Get six to eight hours of sleep every night!

In closing:

The road to living and maintaining a healthy life has not and will not be the easiest road to travel. It is a courageous road paved by trial and error, bumps and bruises, as well as setbacks and struggles. But with every trial and error, I have eagerly discovered. With every bump and bruise, I have graciously healed. And with every setback and struggle, I have victoriously overcome.

Question: What makes me so different?

Answer: Absolutely nothing. I'm no different from you. If I can be successful at changing my life, you can as well ...

Through this amazing journey, I can honestly say that I have grown to love the woman I have become: the woman who vowed to live and maintain a healthier life; the woman who lost 40 lbs of weight in seven months; the woman who has poured out her heart within the pages of this book.; the woman who knows that there is someone else out there in the world who needs to hear these words, "Now is not the time to give up! Get up!"

Who Makes The Rules In Your Life?

"Don't get so caught up in being the person other people want you to be that you lose sight of who you truly are."

People have said, "You are a doctor and doctors are supposed to only associate and socialize with other doctors."

And I said, "I am no better than you or anyone else. So I'll pass on the advice. I make the rules in my life."

God Didn't Make Bifocals Just For Grumpy Old Men

"Stop zooming in and focusing on what other people have going on in their lives. Learn to focus on what you need to do to improve your present and future life."

"OUCH! My tooth hurts!" exclaimed Mr. Eddie as he repeatedly pointed to his swollen face. It was a rainy Wednesday afternoon, and Mr. Eddie had come in for his annual dental exam. Mr. Eddie was a grumpy old man who always wore a pair of glasses, and he only made an appointment whenever he was experiencing major pain. For some unknown reason, this was usually once a year.

After politely introducing myself, a few of the questions I asked were, "Which tooth is causing you pain? How long has it been bothering you? What medications have you been taking to alleviate the discomfort?"

Mr. Eddie excitedly responded with, "It's this one right here! It's been hurting for a while now, and I've been taking ibuprofen for the pain," as he removed a pair of glasses from his face.

Before turning on my dental light, I grabbed a dark pair of safety glasses to help protect his eyes.

What I had failed to realize was that Mr. Eddie was wearing a second pair of glasses on his face, while still holding the first pair of frames in his left hand.

At that very moment, my inner voice went crazy holding a conversation among itself, "How could I have missed him wearing two pairs of glasses? Why was he wearing two pairs of glasses at the same time? Did he even know that he had two pairs of glasses on?"

I silently whispered to my inner voice, "Hush up! This is really none of your concern."

However, the fact that he had been wearing two pairs of glasses intrigued me.

My lips had spoken before my brain had realized it: "Mr. Eddie, why are you wearing two pairs of glasses?"

Oops!

(Silence)

Mr. Eddie turned his head towards me, half – smiled, and hesitantly said, "I broke my bifocals. So I've been wearing two pairs of glasses. One pair helps me focus on what's up close. The other pair helps me focus on what's far away. It was difficult at first, but I've taught myself how to wear both pairs at the same time."

After sending Mr. Eddie home a happy man, I knew in my heart that I wouldn't see him again until the next time he was in pain. Nevertheless, I couldn't stop thinking about Mr. Eddie wearing both pairs of glasses at the same time and how this could be applied to everyday life.

What if you taught yourself how to wear two pairs of glasses at the same time in your everyday life?

THE CLOSE UP: What if you learned how to zoom in and manage your everyday problems with less anxiety and fear and with more preparation and hope? Do you think that would change anything?

What if you started doing those tasks today that you keep putting off for tomorrow? Would you get more accomplished? Would you be more successful?

What if you started caring less about other people's opinions of the labels on your clothes, purses, shoes, and cars and started caring more about investing in an emergency fund, savings account, or retirement plan? Do you believe you would be better prepared if an unexpected financial problem arose?

What if you had a positive mental attitude instead of always being a *negative Nancy* or a *Debbie downer*? Do you think a more positive outlook could change how you view yourself, your life, and the world? Do you think a more positive outlook would change how the world views you?

What if you willingly reached out a helping hand unto your neighbor? Do you believe it would make him/her a stronger person? Do you believe it would make you a stronger person?

THE FAR AWAY: Sometimes, it's easy to become focused on just your everyday problems that you lose sight of your future. That's where your second set of lens come into play.

What if you paused, re – adjusted your eyes, and focused on your future? Have you ever wondered what the world would be like if each of us slowed down and meditated?

What if someone were to ask you,

"What are your dreams? What is your purpose? Can you name some of the things that you love to do? What do you stand for? What is your definition of success? Are you where you want to be in life? If not, what is missing? Do you have a plan? Is there a backup plan? Where do you hope to be in one year, five years, or ten years? What legacy do you want to leave your children? What if you died tomorrow, would you be proud of your life story?"

Would you be able to give them a meaningful answer instead of the three words, "I don't know"?

But I Didn't Call You Old

"When people don't see things the same way you see them, remind yourself that they are looking from their own perspective."

"Oh, how I just love Monday mornings" was my first thought of the day as I listened to Mrs. Smith whine about how she did not want to have her teeth removed.

"Why can't you just leave them alone? I don't want my teeth pulled!" exclaimed Mrs. Smith as she folded her arms across her chest and poked out her lower lip.

I pointed to her black and white x – rays on the large computer screen and said, "I do understand. But you have a bad infection here."

Mrs. Smith squinted her eyes and scanned them over her x – rays.

"But I don't want my teeth pulled" she repeated in a stern voice.

"I know you don't Mrs. Smith. But there is no way to save your teeth. Here is one treatment option we can consider to replace your teeth" was my response as I handed her a model with a few fake teeth on it.

Mrs. Smith looked down at the model with the partial (the fake teeth).

"A partial! A partial is for old people! I'm not old. Are you calling me old?" she asked.

"Wait! What? No! But I didn't call you old! Mrs. Smith, I don't think you understand how serious this is. You have a really bad infection, and your infection can make you sick. Your infection can possibly spread and kill you. Please listen to me!" I pleaded.

"Kill me. Hmm. Well, give me a couple of days to think about it" she said as she stormed out of the consultation room.

After a day or so had passed, Mrs. Smith returned to the office for another appointment.

"Good morning, Mrs. Smith. So what did you decide?" I asked.

"I am here to have one tooth pulled today. Just ONE tooth. This one right here. And that's it!" she said as she held up her right index finger and tapped on her tooth.

"Sure. No problem" was my response as I draped a napkin over her chest.

And just like magic, her tooth was gone.

"Are you done already? What is that salty taste in my mouth?" she asked while moving her tongue back and forth in the crater of the missing tooth.

"Yes, I am finished. Oh! That's the pus from the infection" was my response as I cleaned the crater and packed it with gauze.

Mrs. Smith gulped.

"Oh really" she said.

Her eyes became saddened as she looked down at the tile floor.

"Hmm. I think I need to have my other teeth taken out today" she whispered.

"Huh?" I uttered.

"I know earlier today, I told you I only wanted to have one tooth taken out. And I noticed you didn't argue with me. You just agreed. And I appreciate that. After tasting that nasty pus, I don't want to risk getting another infection. Will you please take my teeth out?" she asked.

At that moment, you and I both know I had no choice but to politely say, "Sure. No problem."

On the previous Monday, the scent of frustration oozed from my pores as Mrs. Smith rebelled against my treatment recommendations. Although I had done my best to explain the reasons why her teeth needed to be pulled, it seemed as if Mrs. Smith only wanted to do what she wanted to do. In my mind, the decision to remove and replace her teeth seemed so simple; it was the best choice for her overall health. In her mind, the decision to remove and replace her teeth seemed so complex; she would have been agreeing to treatment that she was not ready to accept.

How many times has a similar scenario happened in your life?

A loved one, friend, or stranger had a problem (infection) and asked for your advice (treatment recommendation) on how to solve their problem, and after you presented your recommendation: it seemed as if your advice was absolutely not what they wanted to hear. Do you remember feeling frustrated because you wasted time providing helpful information that really did not seem to matter? Can you recall asking yourself, "Why aren't they listening? Did I make sense? Why did they ask, if they didn't want to know?"?

Whenever a similar scenario happens again, here's what you should keep in mind: life involves both emotions and choices. Although the road to solving a problem may seem simple and straightforward to you, that same road may look complex and crooked to the person experiencing the problem. Therefore, you must attempt to present, listen, and respect:

Step 1: Present your advice or recommendations in a calm manner using a calm tone.

Step 2: Actively listen! Try to understand the arguments or reasons the other person has provided. Imagine yourself in their shoes.

Step 3: Respect that they have the right to decide what they want.

More often than not, putting pressure on someone does not cause them to change their mind or decide in your favor. In many cases, it causes the person to either pull away from you or blame you for the results of their decision (even though they initially asked you for your advice). Usually, it is best to give the person some time and space to reflect on what has been said. In the end, they must live with the consequences of their decision.

In Mrs. Smith case, the final decision for her overall well – being (the removal of her teeth) was made by her at the appropriate time.

The Gift That Keeps On Giving

"Give that which is free: your smile can uplift a mood, your hello can change an attitude, and your hug can heal a heart."

Immediately after pulling a couple of teeth on a patient, she reached out her arms and said, "Doctor, I'm ready for my hug!"

My response was, "Hold on, it's coming! But first I have to put some gauze in your mouth!"

Internal thought: When patients start asking for hugs before their treatment is finished, you must be doing something right.

My heartfelt message is simple:

Some people become embarrassed and/or discouraged when they are not able to financially give as much as they would like to give to the church (including tithes), family and friends, or to those who are in need. But let us not forget that giving is not and should not always be about money. The poorest man can give his children two of the greatest gifts in the world: wisdom and love.

Pause for a moment. Write down two things that you can personally contribute (give back) to the world that does not cost any money? How can these two things help make a difference in the world?

1. _____

2. _____

Extra! Extra! Read All About It!

"Be mindful of the tea you pour out. Your words and actions carry more weight and hold more power than you realize."

The cutest kid came into the office for an appointment on a busy day. Upon entering the treatment room, the conversation went as follows:

Johnny: "Hi, Dr. Register! You must be famous?!"

Me: "Huh? What are you talking about Johnny?"

Johnny: "Dr. Register, you just got to be famous because all these folks around here keep calling your name!"

Me: "Well Johnny, if that's your definition of famous. You know what? You are right. I am!"

The Forever Stamp

"When you value making a difference in someone else's life, you begin to make a difference in your own life!"

A young child asked me to personally autograph his cast. He had broken his arm and had been fitted with a bright colored cast. This moment was extra special because it was the first time I had ever signed a cast. Hopefully the message, "You are very special. Love, Dr. Register" would not only be imprinted in his cast, but also be imprinted in his heart.

47

Who's Afraid of The Big Bad Mosquito?

"The most difficult decisions are the ones that take the most courage to make. Sometimes, you must dig deep inside of yourself to find the courage you thought you never had."

"I remember YOU! Are you gonna brush my teeth today?" asked Jeremiah (a young child) as he hesitantly hopped into the banana colored dental chair.

"Nope! I'm not brushing your teeth today" was my response as I adjusted the side button on the chair to lay him down flat.

"What are you gonna do?" he asked while turning his head back and forth from right to left scanning the room for the one thing most people hate more than paying taxes.

You guessed it! He was searching for the big, long, and scary NEEDLE!

While extending my right index finger and turning my wrist in a circular motion, I informed Jeremiah, "Turn around please. Today, I am going to get rid of the cavity bugs in your teeth. You will feel a tiny mosquito bite pinch."

"MOSQUITO BITE! Oh no! I hate mosquitoes!" Jeremiah shouted as he stretched his eyes open wider than a 100 – yard football field.

"It is not a real mosquito bite silly! I will show you what I mean" was my response as I instructed him to hold out his forearm.

After placing my thumb and index fingers together, I lightly pinched his forearm.

"Oh, that's all you're gonna do?" asked Jeremiah while smiling with amazement.

While nodding my head up and down and stretching my arms out wide, I answered, "Yep, that's the worst part. If you are a big boy, I will make sure you get a nice shiny toy from my big ole' treasure box!"

"That's easy! Well, I'm ready man! I'm ready man! Let's do this! I'm ready man! That's easy!" was his response as he boastfully pumped up his chest and gladly laid back in the chair.

"Now close your eyes tight and open your mouth really wide" were my instructions as I grabbed the 30 – gauge needle and gently poked his inner cheek.

Jeremiah closed his eyes and opened his mouth.

After three seconds…

"AHHHHHHH! No! Uh uh! I want my momma! Uh uh! That hurt! I don't like that!" Jeremiah exclaimed as he immediately opened his eyes and attempted to jump out of the chair.

"Calm down sweetheart! You are okay! Let us try it one more time. We will see if the mosquito bite feels a little bit better the second time around!" I pleaded as my dental assistant and I tried to calm him down.

At that very moment, Jeremiah had to make one of the biggest decisions of his young life.

Jeremiah had to decide if having cavity free teeth and receiving a toy were more valuable to him than simply giving up. Of course if Jeremiah was to make the decision to give up, the short – term result (going home without any pain) would seem better than the long – term repercussions (cavities, toothache, infection).

Just as in Jeremiah's life, there will be times in which you only have a few minutes to make a decision that will affect you for a lifetime. Throughout life, you will be faced with important decisions, overwhelming problems, or unforeseen obstacles (the mosquito bites) that will cause you to ask yourself the questions, "Do I try it again?" or "Do I just give up?"

How you decide to handle each of the previously mentioned situations (the mosquito bites) will determine what happens next in your life. Sometimes, the hopes of acquiring or maintaining a specific reward will be involved in your decision – making process, and you will have to determine if the reward (such as a promotion, relationship, money, pride, recognition, social acceptance, or success) is enough incentive to keep you pushing forward.

Sometimes no matter what the reward is, it may not be enough to motivate you to continue down the same path. During this time, you will have to set your fears aside, make a conscious decision to stop continuing down the same road, and take a chance with something else, something different, or something new.

Each decision that you make involves inner strength, courage, wisdom, and faith (internal power). And with each decision, you must remain hopeful, keep an open mind, and be willing to accept the consequences of your choice.

In Jeremiah's case, the hope of a brand new shiny toy gave him the courage needed to continue and finish his dental treatment. After selecting his toy from the treasure box, he wrapped his arms around my waist, placed his head on my stomach, and said, "I was a big boy! That was easy."

Where Are You From?

"You may cross paths with someone whose purpose is to teach a lesson or deliver a message. Be receptive ..."

Early one Thursday morning, I asked a woman a simple question. I asked her, "Ma'am. Where are you from?"

This was the first time I had ever seen or met the woman. She had traveled several miles across the state of Georgia for a dental visit. The woman's name was Ms. Ruby Jane Clayton. She was an older woman with a stoic demeanor. After pondering on my question for a brief moment, Ms. Ruby Jane sharply responded with, "Why do you need to know my business?"

I gulped.

7 seconds of silence ... 8 seconds of silence ... 9 seconds

During this period of silence, I asked myself, "Do you really want to know the answer?"

"I'm sorry. I didn't mean to be nosy. I was just curious. That's all. You're right. It's not any of my business" I uttered as my voice cracked like a teenage boy going through puberty.

"Humph! I'm from a small town." she stated as she pursed her lips and stared out of the window.

At the end of her visit, Ms. Ruby Jane decided to tell me the name of the small town.

"Oh! Wow! My mother is from that same town" I replied.

She tilted her head in the direction of my voice. She grinned as hard as a child who had been left a crisp five dollar bill from the tooth – fairy. "Really? Who are your people?" Mrs. Ruby Jane asked with curiosity.

I informed her of my family's name in a more natural voice.

She placed her right hand over her chest, leaned her head back, and laughed with Jesus. "Lawd! I know your people baby. I knew your grandma. And I knew your granddaddy too. They lived right down the road from us. They were such good people."

After hearing her response, the wells of my eyes filled with an immeasurable amount of tears. Tears of both happiness and sadness rolled down my face. I was happy that she had such wonderful things to say about my grandparents, but I was also sad because I never got a chance to meet my mother's mother or father. Both of her parents died before I was born. During my life, I had only seen one picture of my grandfather and had never seen a picture of my grandmother. I could only imagine what his voice sounded like, what she looked like, and what our relationships would have been like if we had met here on Earth.

Nevertheless, I will forever be grateful she decided to answer such a simple question such as, "Where are you from?" Life is such an amazing journey … you never know who you may meet!

Chapter 3:

Friendship and Community

Closer Than A Brother

"Some people enter your life for only a short season. Some people leave without giving you a reason. But keep in mind, the people who are meant to stay, they stay forever. "

Beautiful things have happened when I have taken the time to get to know people. I must be honest; some of my best friends are people I initially misjudged. It was as if my mind had predetermined that I did not like someone before I even gave that person a fair chance.

Once I opened up my heart, I realized that it's the character on the inside of a person that touches and changes your life forever. And unless you take the time to get to know a person, you won't ever find out what is on the inside.

Just because two individuals have different races, religions, lifestyles, opinions, perspectives, or backgrounds does not mean that they have not been through similar experiences. Two people can also go through shared life experiences that keep them connected for a lifetime.

Whether they live close by one another or are separated by thousands of miles of physical distance, genuine friends have emotional hearts that will always and forever be invisibly tied together.

Luckily for me, the people that I misjudged were open and willing to give me an opportunity to become their friend.

The Hardest Fight Of Our Lives

"Your life shouldn't involve you just praying and fighting for yourself, it should involve you praying and fighting for others too."

For eighteen years,

Sarah and I have been BEST friends

We first met and studied French together

We graduated high school together

We went to college together

We achieved professional degrees together

We stumbled through our fair share of relationships together

We lived in and explored the big city together

We have experienced life's journey together

and we …

WE will fight cancer TOGETHER!

Please join me in a special prayer of healing for Sarah. I love her with all of my heart!

No One Could Have Told Me

"Never forget to thank those who have held your hand, wiped your tears, or offered you a shoulder to lean on in times of need."

Ten years ago …

Lorraine and I met at the College of Dental Medicine. She was a dental assistant, and I was a dental student.

Ten years ago …

No one could have told me that I would meet an assistant that would forever change my life.

Ten years ago …

No one could have told me that there would be another person in this world besides my mother that would be cheering, praying, and encouraging me to push through dental school as well as life.

After successfully graduating, I moved two and a half hours away. She had been telling me for seven years, "I'm coming to visit you one day!"

Well yesterday, she finally made it.

We laughed and talked just like the good ole' days.

Everything felt as though nothing in life had ever changed.

But after she left, my eyes fought to hold back tears as I reflected on our lives.

Ten years ago …

Ten years ago, no one could have told me that I would meet one of my best friends.

Someone Else Lives Within Me

"There will be times when you have to pick up the baton and run for those who cannot run. Someone is counting on you!"

Today, I found out
A young woman I went to college with had passed away
We were two of few African – American students to graduate with professional degrees

To be honest, I think we may have been
the only two African – American students in the program at that time

She was one year ahead of me in the program,
so we really didn't get a chance to see each other much

But secretly, she was my inspiration

Her passion for success was contagious
Her determination to succeed made me even more determined to succeed

Although the program was hard, I just couldn't give up
I couldn't give up, because she wasn't giving up
If she could persevere, guess what? I could too.

Today, I found out
A young woman I went to college with had passed away

But her fighting spirit … it still lives within me

And she,
She will always be
She will forever be
MY ENDLESS INSPIRATION

Can We Be Beautiful?

"You are here on Earth for only a short period of time. Help build a legacy that the next generation can carry forward."

Change! It begins with each of us making a conscious decision to not make the same mistakes we made yesterday.

Change continues when we realize that although each of our physical lives are different: we all have a voice that matters, we all have a life story that is important, and we all serve a Creator that is just!

Change spreads with the decision of holding hands to pray instead of holding guns to riot. It's the choice of standing in line at the precinct to vote instead of simply sitting at home on the sofa complaining about change. It's the amazing ability to pause, look ahead into our future, and see the end result of our action before it actually happens.

We as a nation have the freedom to pray, right to vote, power to love, strength to forgive, and choice to make a positive difference in the lives of our children, loved ones, friends, and mere strangers!

Change! It can be such a meaningful, monumental, and noble decision! But folks, it has to start somewhere. So why not start with the efforts of both you and me?

We Lead By Example

"You cannot change the whole world, but you can help make a difference. Let your light shine!"

Why are we here?

We are not here to push our beliefs off on anyone else. We are here to tell our stories. Stories of who we are. Stories of what we have been through. Stories of hope.

When we try to force our beliefs on other people, we often come off pushy and overzealous; which turns people off and pushes them further away.

Let us lead by example: with compassion, tolerance, benevolence, and love. For, the man with the highest integrity and most noble character is not always the most religious man.

Our lips proclaim that we are a Christian, but let us ask ourselves, "Do our actions show others that we are Christ – like?"

Do we even understand what it means to be, "Christ – like"?

Simply proclaiming we are a Christian doesn't make us any different than anyone else, but treating all people with a genuine and loving spirit does.

We are a community of united voices that should be working together to promote good in this world.

Our stories are a powerful instrument. They should not be told to mislead or hurt others. They should be spoken to inform and educate. They should be told to inspire and uplift!

When we make a commitment to ourselves to become better people; we help other people become better people. We lead by example!

People don't have to know every detail about us to recognize a difference within us. Choosing to do what's right doesn't always make us popular. But it does make us feel good. And that good feeling can't ever be taken away.

And that is why WE are here …

An Army of Words

"God didn't make only you in His image; He made each one of us in His image. Give unto others the same respect that you desire."

I painfully gave birth to my words
Innocent letters born into a callous world
Letters united to form an army of words
Valiant words whispering in the silence of night
Echoing in a voice of unity: NO VIOLENCE
Words never drinking
from the river of fury

I painfully gave birth to my words
Innocent letters born into a callous world
Letters united to form an army of words
Noble words rebelling against the direction of the wind
Echoing in a voice of unity: NO INTOLERANCE
Words never drinking
from the river of judgment

I painfully gave birth to my words
Innocent letters born into a callous world
Letters united to form an army of words
Courageous words shouting in the silence of the night
Echoing in a voice of unity: NO RACISM
Words never drinking
from the river of condemnation

I painfully gave birth to my words
Innocent letters born into a callous world

Letters united to form an army of words
Fearless words dancing against the direction of the wind
Echoing in a voice of unity: NO HATE
Words never drinking from the river of death

Macaroni and Cheese Isn't So Bad

"A community becomes family, a team becomes champions, and a nation becomes heroes when they work together for the greater good. Now is the time to do your part: big or small!"

Who's ever met a dentist who didn't love to talk? Well there may be a few party poopers out there, but I'm certainly not one of them. While at the office, I absolutely adore talking to my patients about everything under the sun. There aren't many topics I can't or won't talk about. My patients and I indulge in daily conversations about life, travel, news, fashion, entertainment, sports, food, and let me dare not forget: teeth.

Not too long ago, a patient and I were discussing foods that each of us disliked. And anyone who really knows me knows there is one food I absolutely dislike the taste of: *macaroni and cheese.* So of course, I didn't have a problem telling her it was my least favorite food. And she didn't bite her tongue responding back with, "Doc, you aren't really Southern if you don't like macaroni and cheese."

"What?" My southern accent and ego had both been insulted.

Who could be anymore Southern than I was?

I was born and raised on a farm in the deepest part of Georgia. If you go any further South, well if you stayed awake in geography class, you know where you would end up. Obviously, she didn't know that I had grown up alongside chickens, hogs, and goats. Obviously, she didn't know I had tasted fruit from the trees of the Garden of Eden. And yes the fruit was delicious! At that very moment, she had me questioning my own "Southern – icity."

After hours of reflection, I did what any normal person would do. I went home and pulled out my laptop to do a bit of research. It was time to take this to social media. Login. Type. Post. Too late. It was done.

My post was pretty simple. It read, 'A patient said, "Doc, you really aren't Southern if you don't like macaroni and cheese." Do you like macaroni and cheese? Yes or No.'

After minutes of hearing nothing but crickets, people began posting their responses. There were a handful of folks who said they didn't like it at all. Most said that they did. Some agreed they liked to eat it hot! Some said they liked to eat it cold! People reported they liked it with bacon. Two or three agreed they liked it with lobster. Some said the more cheese the merrier. A few said they liked theirs covered with ranch dressing.

RANCH DRESSING! My tongue just quivered!

There were those who believed it was so delicious and nutritious that it should be classified as a vegetable. And there were those who couldn't deny enjoying it but reported staying away from it because it went straight to their butt. *Hmm!* It all makes sense now, that's the reason why I don't have one. Forgive me! I digress!

Who knew that one simple food would make women question their parenting skills in response to their teenagers' true confession of not liking it after many years of preparation? I felt so sorry for those poor kids; confessions to momma are never easy.

Almost 90 – 100 comments later, it really didn't matter that those in favor of the faint colored noodles topped with yellow, creamy cheese had dominated and won the vote. For minutes, I just sat on my bed staring at my screen with great amazement. I was in awe of the beauty of people from all over the country with different backgrounds, religious views, purposes, values, economic classes, and races uniting as a community to express their individual beliefs with humor, honesty, and respect.

If people as a whole, would listen to each other, respect one another, and work together to achieve common dreams, then our society, nation, and world would be a much more peaceful place. *Hmm?* With the hope of greater world peace and good will, well maybe, just maybe, macaroni and cheese isn't so bad after all.

My Heart Shed Tears

"Some people spend their time wishing they had someone else's life; not realizing that someone else is wishing they had their life. Give thanks for what you have at the moment."

My heart shed tears
As I listened to the story of the man
Who lost most of what he had
House, car, and friends
Peace, pride, and joy
as a result of one unforeseen misfortune

My eyes shed tears
As I listened to the story of the mother
diagnosed with an incurable cancer
raising three young children on her own
not ready to leave her children
alone here on this earth

My ears shed tears
As I listened to the story of the child
who willingly took his own life
after years of being bullied
laughed at and ridiculed
just because he did not look and act a certain way

My lips shed tears
As I listened to the story of the woman
mentally and physically traumatized
after being abused

by her unfaithful boyfriend
of one and a half years

My heart shed tears
Tears of empathy
As I listened to each of their testimonies and life stories

My heart shed tears
Tears of appreciation
As I am reminded that my life
With all of its pain, disappointments, mishaps, and mistakes
Is worthy to be cherished, respected, celebrated, and lived

My heart shed tears
Tears of gratitude
For this precious gift called *LIFE*

Chapter 4:

Forgiveness and Love

The Art of Forgiveness

"You will miss out on some of the best moments of life if you aren't willing to ask for, offer, and receive forgiveness."

There was once a time when I was too ashamed to call upon God and ask Him for His forgiveness (repentance). How could I ask the Almighty Creator to forgive me of my sins, especially when I was not willing to forgive myself? I had read within the books of Psalms and Ephesians that God was rich in mercy. I knew from the books of Romans and Ecclesiastes that no one was perfect. But I often felt ashamed and guilty of my shortcomings. Somehow my pride had convinced me that I was different from everyone else inhabiting this Earth. And because I was different, I was always supposed to know and do better.

I also struggled with asking others for forgiveness. Sometimes, it was because I was too embarrassed to admit that I was wrong. Other times, my ego just wouldn't let me do it. And there were times when I just wasn't sure of how the other person was going to respond to my apology. There were instances when I had sincerely apologized and the other person made the decision not to forgive me. And as a result, my pride grew overprotective of my heart.

Many times, I do believe I was too eager to forgive. I had allowed the same people to repeat the same mistakes over and over again. As if the words, "I'm sorry" were all that was needed for me to give them a third, fourth, or fifth chance even though their actions did not speak as loudly as their words.

Over time, life has taught me that forgiveness takes ***effort***.

It takes putting my ego (pride) aside and evaluating the whole picture. It involves apologizing when I have erred in order to make matters between me and a loved one better. It means understanding that everyone isn't going to accept my apology no matter how many times I genuinely ask for their forgiveness. It requires making some tough decisions such as forgiving someone and giving them another chance (holding on) versus forgiving someone and moving on with my life (letting go).

Over time, life has taught me that forgiveness is an ***art***.

It is an art that has to be practiced. Practiced and practiced, over and over. It's a choice: a choice that takes willingness. When I allowed my mind to accept that we all are human and we all make mistakes, it made forgiving myself, forgiving others, asking for forgiveness from God, and asking for forgiveness from others easier. It gave my frantic soul a sense of peace. But I still had to keep in mind, just because mistakes are inevitable does not mean that I shouldn't hold myself and others accountable. Accountability is essential for both forgiveness and growth.

The Eyes of Our Soul

"The road to change begins with the first step. Sometimes, the smallest step can have the biggest impact. You have to start somewhere."

Emotions, frustrations, confrontations, and situations

Can often lead us down a pathway

An erroneous pathway, never meant to be traveled

And we sometimes forget about the true happiness we shared with our loved one, prior to the situation

And we begin to let anger

Fuel our motivation

Oh, this intensifying anger

It can cause us to express

Our individualized words

With such passion and deep rage

That during that moment ... instance ... second

The love we possessed for the other person seems to disappear

But thereafter,

After our adrenaline rush has come to an end

It is then ... that

The eyes of our soul become awakened

And we realize

We have made a mistake

And simultaneously,

Our suppressed feelings, good intentions, and undying love reappear

Hoping and praying that our loved one is stronger

And willing to FORGIVE ...

A Copper Penny In Your Eyes

"It's the most difficult moments in life that show you where you are in faith, strength, and courage."

I welcomed you to be my friend

But it was you who chose not to

I didn't even know you

Well enough to not like you

Made up in your mind

Decision to simply ignore me

A copper penny in your eyes

Much too cheap to be recognized

A vinyl album in your ears

Much too old to be heard

Silenced by your words

My Glory refused not to shine

Abused by your tone

My Glory still refused not to shine

Hurt by your rejection

My Glory willed and refused not to shine

Now, I am needed by you

Well,

I've made up my mind

I've chosen

Not to be your friend

Glory and I

We've made it this far

Without you

Twenty – One Love Notes

"Open your heart and mind in preparation for love, so that when it happens: both will be ready."

Ahh, love. It's one of those magical connections in life that we all desire to have. Some people seem to have more success with it than others. As for me, I went through fourteen years of disappointment and loneliness before I finally realized that true love began with me first. After several unsuccessful attempts at trying to make relationships work with the wrong people, I had to start over and honestly evaluate my expectations of others as well as my expectations of myself. How could I expect another human being to love me, when I didn't love me? My love life changed (for the better) once I took a chance on the one person who should have always mattered the most – **me**. Below you will find 21 invaluable lessons I have learned about love and relationships throughout the years.

1. Quit telling yourself that there is something wrong with you. There is absolutely nothing wrong with you. You are beautiful on the inside and out. It just takes some people longer than others to find the right one who connects with them.

2. Stop expecting the right one to just show up at your front door. In order to meet the right one, you must be willing to put yourself out there. You must become social.

3. There is nothing wrong with being single. Spending quality time alone with yourself is just as important as spending quality time with others. Rejuvenation is essential.

4. Before you can teach other people how to treat you, you must first determine how you want to be treated.

5. You have to love and place value on yourself: know your worth. No one can do it for you, give it to you, find it for you, or buy it for you.

6. Knowing what you will not tolerate in a relationship is just as important as knowing what you will.

7. If someone says, "I don't want a relationship" then that means, "They don't want a relationship." Take their word at face value. Don't waste your time hoping they will change their mind, because it's highly unlikely that they will. Next …

8. When someone truly cares about you, they make time for you. Point. Blank. Period. They call you. They answer your texts. They want to spend quality time with you. "I've been busy" is just an excuse.

9. Your intuition knows whether or not someone is treating you right. If someone isn't treating you the way you deserved to be treated, find someone else who will.

10. Don't get caught up in your feelings. If you meet someone and they don't keep their word, chances are they won't start. Move on! It's a lot easier to move on in the early stages.

11. Giving a person too much too soon still doesn't make a person want to be in a relationship. Slow down!

12. Your dignity is your most prized possession. Protect it. Treat it like gold. Don't let anyone ever take it away from you.

13. Don't suppress your feelings: How you feel about something matters just as much as how the other person feels. Don't be afraid to communicate.

14. If you let people know what's important to you, and they act like they don't care: change the company you keep.

15. Change begins with you first. Some people spend their lives hoping for the other person to change. In order for change to happen, you may have to change who or what you want.

16. If you are willing to put up with anything, people will continue to give you anything.

17. When you turn a blind eye to all of the red flags, blindness and disappointment will surely follow.

18. You shouldn't have to beg a person to be a part of your life. There are too many people searching for someone like you.

19. If you keep telling yourself that there aren't any good men/women out there, eventually you will start to believe it. There are plenty of good people in this world.

20. If a relationship is not fulfilling your needs, moving on is best. It may not feel good at the moment, but you will be glad you did in the future. (sigh of relief)

21. A man/woman who confirms his/her love not only with his/her lips but also by his/her actions is a man/woman after your heart.

Nothing But Hope

"Just because you meet someone doesn't mean that he/she is the right one for you. Be patient ..."

Child ...

You've only known him for

4 weeks

6 days

9 hours

14 minutes and

22 seconds

And you're this sad already

If you're this sad

and you didn't have sex with him

Just imagine how you would really feel

If you did

Child please ...

That sadness that you say you feel

It ain't nothing but ole' Hope

Hope that YOU eagerly put into the situation

And now your Hope got you shame

Got you shedding tears

Got you feeling all sorry for yourself

But *Child* …

Just be patient

Don't you let ole' Hope steal your Joy

You've got TOO much going for yourself

GOD has given you too many blessings

For your lips and soul not to smile

My Fruit Feels Unworthy

"Pretending something isn't happening doesn't solve the problem. You have to be real (honest) with yourself in order to move forward."

It was love at **hello**,

His tongue bled red words that made

my heart feel as though he wanted to love me

Red words that flowed through my veins connecting

and pumping dopamine into

the translucent places and transparent spaces

that filled my dreams with hope

Dreams of finally getting *HIM* right

Hopes of connecting with the man who understood that all I wanted

from this world was to be loved

And to give love

Love that was so strong

it could cause my being to explode

if it had not been kept cool by my fear of being rejected

Love that was so strong

it caused my being to explode

when his red words revealed that he never loved me

And now my fruit feels **unworthy**

Love that was so strong

it caused my being to explode

due to his unwillingness to act

Ignored phone calls and unanswered texts

His tongue bled red words that made

my heart feel as though he couldn't dare to love me

Red words that flowed through my veins connecting

and pumping cortisol into

the intense places and painful spaces that

filled my dreams with hope

Dreams of making *US* right

Hoping that he would awaken so that we could

pick up the broken pieces and

continue on in September, October, or November from

where we left off

But we could **not** ...

It was a love that was so strong

it caused my being to explode

If his tongue had not bled red words

It was pain at **goodbye**

The Night My Lips First Spoke

"You're stronger today than you were yesterday. You'll be stronger tomorrow than you were today. Strength is gained with experience and time."

For years,

Silence was the only word my lips ever spoke

Tears were the only sound my ears ever heard

Sorrow was the only beat my heart ever felt

And yet, I loved you more yesterday

More than I loved myself

But the woman who lived inside of me

She was alone

So many lies and so much deceit

Why was this happening to me

Anger and shame

Laughter no longer knew my first name

Pain and fear

They could no longer reside here

Strength and prayer

This was my life, I had to care

Dignity and hope

Without you, my heart was determined to still cope

Freedom and peace

A fearless woman now lives inside of me

There's a woman who lives inside of me

Who's stronger than I could ever imagine

The woman who lived inside of me

She is now gone

How An Angel Changed My Love Life

"An unsuccessful relationship with the wrong person will make you appreciate a successful relationship with the right person."

Christmas 2013: On our last day of work, Molly walked into my office and stretched out her arms. Our faces lit up with excitement as we gave each other our annual hug goodbye. After six minutes of chit – chat on how each of us was spending our holiday break, she walked out into the cold to enjoy her time off with family. I, on the other hand, had at least another half hour of paperwork to finish. My day had gone as planned. It always started with an endless number of patients and it always ended with an endless amount of paperwork. It was the life of a dentist. But I didn't mind. I was young and single without a child or husband. Lucky enough to already had experienced my fair share of *bad* relationships; I appreciated the idea of spending some time alone with just my computer.

After a couple of minutes of typing at my desk, a faint voice knocked at my door. It was once again, Molly. As she walked through the door, she said with some hesitation, "Dr. Register, please excuse me for bothering you again. I know you haven't shared anything like this with me before, but God told me to tell you something. He said, 'You'll know that you've met the right one when things are easy and not hard.' "

And folks let me tell you, she made the hairs on the back of my neck tremble. I was so used to the *hard* in relationships, that my brain wouldn't dare allow me to imagine the *easy*.

From that day forth, figuring out the *easy* became my mission. Books and articles on personal growth, relationships, and success became my inner soul's food. My soul was hungry! It had been starving for a three course meal of home cooked knowledge! The more I read, the more I reflected on my strengths and flaws.

Reading and reflecting both gave me a better understanding of who I was on the inside; the meaning of self – value, self – acceptance, and self – love. They allowed me to better understand the type of person I wanted in my life (example: someone who desired to get married). They helped me to recognize and prevent some of the same mistakes I'd made in the past (example: no longer dating someone who wanted a casual relationship when I knew that I wanted to be in a committed relationship). And they helped me to recognize the type of person that wanted someone like me in their life.

Christmas 2014: On our last day of work, I found myself thinking about all of the happiness I had experienced throughout the entire year. I was amazed at how one person's message could change the way you see yourself, your life, and the world. By the way, earlier this year I met someone who absolutely loves to make me smile. Unfortunately this past Christmas, Molly and I missed out on our annual hug. And I must admit, it made me sad. I'd been waiting for that special moment to tell my angel the words, "Thank You."

Rhythm of Your Heart

"Remember, the right one accepts you for who you are and appreciates all of the gifts that you bring to the table."

Wait.

Wait for the ONE who is willing to show your heart that they can be trusted. They understand that although they have not given you a reason not to trust them that maintaining your trust is:

Important.

Critical.

Essential to your well – being.

It is the beat of your heart.

Wait for the ONE who recognizes that trust gives you the permission to be:

Complete.

Whole.

Comfortable in your own skin.

Trust brings out the best in you.

Wait for the ONE who understands that trust gives you the courage to be more vulnerable and beautiful.

It allows you to be who you truly are,

your authentic self: original.

Wait for the ONE who knows that trust has the power to sync your heartbeat with theirs:

Two hearts beating as one.

Connected.

Forever by trust.

Wait for the ONE …

Just wait.

In Flaming Hot Love

"A strong relationship takes both people putting in their fair share of work in order to see successful results. It takes two!"

Words thrown like hand grenades

Back and forth across their lips

No one heard a single word

All they heard was tick tick

Red fire sparkled in his eyes

His ego ignited

Bloody anger boiled within his veins

His pride exploded

Intense fear fluttered through her heart

Her voice pleaded

Salty liquid streamed from her eyes

Her spirit melted

Flaming hatred ached within their bones

Their love battled

Passionate forgiveness tugged at their feet

Their souls repented

Love thrown like hand grenades

Back and forth across their lips

No one remembered a single word

Chapter 5:

Family and Hope

_____

Dust Off Your Knees

"When you fall down: choose to get up, dust off your knees and run again. Don't ever give up. The finish line is too close!"

Life is so unique in that although we all walk this journey hand in hand, each person's roadmap is individually different: this includes strangers, friends, as well as family. After reading the final pieces: close your eyes, open your mind, and think back on the special memories of your life that will remain embedded in the hidden parts of your heart forever. These memories are the ones that make your imperfect journey worth finishing.

Pause for a moment. Write down three memories (from childhood through adulthood) that you will never forget.

1. _____

2. _____

3. _____

How did each memory influence you?

1. _____

2. _____

3. _____

Here's My Dirty Little Secret

"Success isn't handed out. It isn't given. It's earned by those who want it. If you aren't willing to do the work, success may not be for you."

Ever since my cousin was born, he and I have always had a close relationship. We are ten years apart, and I am the oldest. Being the oldest, I have always tried to be a good role model for him. His success has always been just as important to me as my success.

From grade school to dental school, I have always been a bit of a perfectionist: I graduated within the top one percent of my high school class, I graduated within three years with a bachelor's degree in chemistry, and I made all A's on my clinical boards required to obtain my dental license. By no means am I trying to brag. But nothing was given to me! I had to put in the work for everything I got.

My cousin on the other hand he has always been the "just let me get by kind of guy." While this type of mindset worked for him in high school. Now that he is in college, it is a different type of ball game. As a result, he loves to blame everyone for him not being successful. It is the teacher's fault because he chose to play video games instead of study. It is the advisor's fault because he did not pay attention in his computer class. It is the financial aid department's fault because he did not submit his financial aid application prior to the deadline. It is the sky's fault because it is blue. It's the grass' fault because it is green.

Blah, blah, blah, blah, blah ... "BLAH!" Sorry! That last one was built up deep down on the inside. I hope you were able to cover your ears.

Finally, it is time for me to share my dirty little secret with my cousin and anyone else who desires to succeed: You cannot live your life blaming others for you not succeeding. Well you can, but unfortunately it will not get you very far. Your success is not another person's responsibility. Well, whose is it?

It's your own!

FIRST! You must make up your mind that you CAN and WILL succeed. Let your internal power and determination fuel the way. Be willing to do whatever it takes: legally and morally.

That simply means be willing to do your work: going back to school to pursue a higher level of education (at any age), staying up late to study for an exam, reviewing that dang ole' hard calculus, putting in multiple applications for a better job, realizing that now is not the time to buy another pair of shoes, working hours of overtime to save for your future, learning how to become a better leader, and practicing, practicing, and practicing your craft.

Oh! By the way! Did I mention, "*Practicing your craft*"?

The examples are endless ... Life's journey may become more difficult with time, but you must remember there are alternative routes to achieve your dreams. At the end of the day, your destination is **success.** It is my belief that you can be great, but it is your decision to become GREAT!

Why Do You Write?

"Never be afraid to tell your personal story. Your words may breathe new life into someone who has lost all hope."

One evening while on the telephone, a friend asked, "Why do you write?"

"I was just curious. It seems pretty boring to me. I can think of a million other interesting things to do instead of writing" she added.

At that time, I wasn't sure whether to feel insulted or to answer her question. I had never thought of the reasons why my lungs yearned to write. I just knew that it was a recreational activity that gave me pleasure just as others enjoyed throwing a ball through a hoop, watching two grown men fake wrestle on cable, or listening to political poppycock on the late night news.

For weeks, I meditated on my friend's question, "Why do you write?"

Hmm, I write because ...

Eleven years ago, I had my first panic attack. A panic attack is a sudden feeling of intense anxiety and fear that causes your brain to think you are dying. At least that is what mine felt like.

One night as I laid on my mother's queen size bed, I experienced one of the most terrifying moments of my life. A warm and tingling sensation covered my entire body. I started to strip out of my clothes from head to toe to escape this foreign sensation. As I attempted to remove my shirt, my head felt as dizzy as a drunkard attempting to pass a walk and turn sobriety test.

My breathing became more shallow and rapid. I was fearful that the oxygen to my lungs would be cut off at any given second. My mind was afraid that my eyes would become blackened, my ears would become deaf, and my heartbeat would no longer dance to the rhythm of life. In my mind someone was switching my power button to the off position, and I was desperately fighting to keep the switch on. I remember begging God not to end my life at that time. My lips kept repeating the words, "I'm not ready to leave yet. I still have so much work to do here on Earth."

Was this my time to die?

After hearing my voice echo throughout the house, my mother quickly dialed 911. And to be honest, I don't remember who was more afraid. When the ambulance arrived, I immediately asked one of the paramedics, "Am I about to die?"

"No, you aren't going to die. All of your vital signs are okay. It seems you may have experienced a panic attack" he answered with a smile.

"A panic attack! What is a panic attack? And why did it happen to me?" I wondered while lying helplessly on the stretcher with a face full of oxygen.

The emergency room doctor agreed with the paramedic, they both believed that I had experienced a sudden panic attack. After being released from the emergency room, an intense feeling of fear fermented deep within my stomach. I wasn't sure when or where this "panic attack" monster would rear its ugly head again.

My mother soon scheduled me an appointment to see a therapist. After listening to my recollection of my nightmare, the therapist gave me her diagnosis on a single sheet of white paper imprinted with three black words, "Generalized Anxiety Disorder." Since I was headed off to dental school in the fall, she also wrote me a prescription for an anxiety medication to help calm my rambunctious nerves.

Each morning before class, I faithfully popped a tiny white pill in my mouth: a tiny white pill that made me so sleepy, I could barely stay awake during class; a tiny white pill that sent electrical sensations throughout my body at any random moment; a tiny white pill that I had been in a secret relationship with for four very long years.

After graduating from dental school, my therapist and I decided it was time to end my long – term affair with my anxiety medication. With time, I slowly divorced the tiny white pill. I gradually learned how to manage my anxiety via stress management techniques: meditation, exercise, and writing.

Hmm, I write because …

I write because writing has been my therapy. Writing has given my soul a **voice**: a creative expression of my thoughts and emotions. An eternal voice that will live on this Earth forever, even after my physical body is no longer here.

Writing has given my soul **courage**: the internal strength needed to paint a colorful portrait of my life with splashes of life – changing experiences, tattoos of my character and beliefs, and brush – strokes of my innermost fears. Writing has helped me to identify past events that have shaped and molded me into the woman I am today.

Writing has given my soul a **purpose**: an external mission to help heal myself as well as others through the use of words. It has allowed me to passionately shout unto the world, "Never be ashamed of who you are. Never be embarrassed of the experiences you have gone through. Each unique challenge you have faced has made you stronger than you were in the past. Your deepest, darkest, and scariest fears can be overcome. You are never alone. We will travel this journey together. Our work is not done here on Earth."

Hmm, I write because …

I write because I must breathe. (exhales)

When Good Enough Becomes Never Enough

"A poor man can feel as though he has more than enough while a rich man can feel as though he never has enough. Success is a mindset."

Over the past sixteen years I have graduated from college, worked as a chemist, attended dental school, and practiced dentistry. The past sixteen years have been an adventurous roller – coaster ride filled with joy as well as pain, smiles with a lot of tears, hope with a few regrets, and failures overcome by victory.

When I think about my life ... What message has guided me through the years?

I wasn't born rich. My family was poor. In my world, there was no silver spoon, no two – story house, no white picket fence, and no dog named, *Buddy*. I was raised on a farm by a mother who took care of five people on an elementary school teacher's salary. For many years, we lived in the same blue trailer and drove the same blue car.

There were times when we had no gas to cook food, there were times when we had no heat to stay warm, and there were times when we had no air to stay cool. There were many times when mother struggled to make ends meet. But she never lost **hope**.

She was determined. She always made sure we had food on our table, clothes on our backs, and love in our hearts. She was grateful. She was thankful for the all of the gifts we did have and never seemed to worry about other people's opinions of her or our family.

One life lesson I would like to share with you is a lesson I learned (at an early age) from my mother: "Never look to the left. Never look to the right. Just always stay focused. And keep looking straight ahead." These words have successfully carried me through the years. They have guided me through some of the most difficult times of my life: times where I just felt like giving up. But I couldn't.

My Heartfelt Message:

Many people spend their whole lives trying to "keep up with the Joneses" (looking left or right). Don't spend your life focusing on what other people surrounding you have going on. Stop comparing yourself and what you have to others and what they have. It takes a whole lot of energy to worry. And worry and jealousy drain the mind and body causing mental and physical problems in the long run.

Whenever you put all of your energy into worrying about what other people have, you lose sight of your own goals, dreams, or desires. When you lose sight of your own hopes, good enough becomes ***never enough***. You get to the point, where you are unable to truly enjoy the gifts and treasures that you have worked so hard to achieve.

Two Keys to a Happier Life:
Determination and Gratefulness

Determination: Simply putting in the effort to achieve the goals you desire to accomplish in life.

Gratefulness: Simply appreciating what you have worked hard to achieve in life.

The Unexpected Heroine

"You don't have to be a fan of math to remember the most important rule: Always count your blessings!"

July 2013: It was the day after my younger brother's birthday. My younger sister went into preterm labor and gave birth to my niece earlier than her obstetrician had anticipated. My niece was born three months prematurely. Nevertheless, she was the most beautiful baby I had ever laid eyes on. She was also the smallest baby that I had ever held in my arms. Weighing approximately two lbs, her tiny pamper was almost bigger than she was.

Although my niece had a fighting spirit, she like many premature babies suffered from a condition called Gastroesophageal Acid Reflux Disease (GERD).

What causes GERD?

The valve between her stomach and esophagus was weak and did not work properly causing her to frequently spit up her water and milk. This frequent regurgitation had to be continually monitored due to a higher risk of aspiration or choking. For up to eighteen months, my sister would have to be mindful of how she was feeding my niece. The pediatrician recommended feeding her smaller meals; burping her frequently during meals; and keeping her in an upright position for at least a half an hour after meals.

November 2013: I happened to be at my mother's home during the Thanksgiving holiday. One evening while spending time with family and friends, I heard my mother yell from a distance, "Help! Help! The baby is choking! She's choking, and she can't breathe!"

My long legs galloped across the front yard faster than Usain Bolt's legs during his record – breaking 100 – meter race. In four months of life, my niece had brought my family closer together than we had ever been.

I'd be darned if she would leave us now.

After grabbing her from my sister's hands, I sat on the edge of my mother's living room couch and briefly looked at her. She looked like a helpless baby doll. Her big gray eyes whispered the words, "Dear Aunty, please save me."

Both of my hands shivered. The vibrations of my heart were stronger than those felt during a 9.0 magnitude earthquake on the Richter scale. The intensity of each heart beat could be detected and measured as far away as Africa.

I placed my left arm on top of my left knee and gently flipped my niece over. Her face rested in the palm of my left hand while her body rested along my long and thin forearm. Her chubby thighs straddled my elbow. As her lifeless body laid there, I raised my right hand and delivered five firm blows to her upper back.

One. Two. Three. Four. Five.

After the series of back blows, I positioned my right palm to help support her head, neck, and back. Using both hands, I carefully turned her over to face me. I rested her body against my right knee. Then,

She started crying …

Hallelujah! My lungs exhaled an immeasurable sigh of relief. From that moment forward, I knew that everything would be okay.

My Heartfelt Message:

Over the past eight years, I have taken a total of four First Aid and Basic Life Support (CPR, Cardiopulmonary Resuscitation) classes. As a healthcare professional (dentist), we are required to have an up to date First Aid and CPR certification every two years. Although I have taken more CPR courses than the average person, you never truly appreciate the importance of hands – on training until it hits close to home.

An emergency is a sudden event that doesn't give you time to come up with a full game plan. Many emergencies such as baby Abby suffocating while sleeping, Uncle Tommy choking on a chicken bone, cousin Chris falling into a swimming pool, or grandma Myrtle experiencing cardiac arrest happen right at home.

First Aid and CPR classes teach you how to quickly and effectively respond when an unexpected emergency situation occurs such as suffocation, choking, drowning, or cardiac arrest. They teach you how to react to someone who is choking; how to respond when someone has stopped breathing; how to treat someone whose heart has stopped beating; and so much more.

I urge you to take a Pediatric and Adult First Aid and CPR class at least once during your lifetime. Emergency treatment for pediatric and adults is not the same. Many organizations offer online and hands – on classes throughout the world that may help you to save a loved one's life. Help spread the word!

I Will Always Love You

"Hold on to those who support you, those who are proud of you, and those who wish to see you succeed: they are your backbone."

Earlier today, I found out my grandmother (my father's mother) had passed away.

She would always tell me, "I'm proud of you baby. Promise me, you'll keep doing good."

"I promise. I will grandma … I will always love you."

Never A Place Like Home

"Sometimes in order to appreciate where you are in life, you have to remind yourself of where you came from."

Her beautiful brown eyes awakened

As her nose twinkled from the smell

Aroma of fresh homemade buttermilk biscuits

Draped with sweet brown cane syrup

Scent of crisp white linen washed in the washer

Hung and dried on the clothes line with faded wooden pins

Site of delicious fruit trees planted in the orchard

Watered each day by the plentiful tears of angels

As they faithfully gave praise to their omnipotent Creator

Fragrance of flowers planted with seeds of hope, seeds of love

Bright and colorful arrangements: reds, yellows, and greens

Golden brown pecans gathered and sold by the bucket

Whistle of a tractor horn amidst the tallest pine trees

Laughter of young children as one hid and the others sought

Sounds of playful dogs barking way off in the distance

White framed windows unlatched and opened wide

Cool breezes of sweet and innocent born memories

There will never ever be a place like home …

The Yellow Sun Has Risen

"You were not put on Earth to be perfect; you were put here for a purpose. You are alive today because there is a meaning, a purpose, a plan for your life. You still have work to do!"

I hung upside down from the branch of self – pity

Buried my troubles deep within my old warped cocoon

And quietly reflected upon my past mistakes

As if worrying about the past

Would make my today a tad bit different

And as I hung from that branch

The weight of my worries

Became too much

Causing me to realize

That if that branch should break

Nothing could be done today

To change my yesterday

For yesterday, yesterday was such a grey dreary day

In my old warped cocoon, I shed so many tears

Remembering the painful regrets in life that made me cry

Crying for the ones who refused to be loved

For yesterday, that branch did break

But today, today the yellow sun has risen

From my old warped cocoon, I began to emerge

Living for the precious moments in life that make me laugh

Laughing with the one who has taught me how to love

Loving the yellow butterfly I have now become

For tomorrow, I shall open up my wings to fly

Our work is not done here on Earth. Stayed tuned as our journey continues ...

Acknowledgments

A special thanks to my mother (Irene) who has believed in me. As a child you taught me how to dream – and to dream big. As a teenager you taught me the importance of education – to put myself in the best position possible. As a young adult you taught me how to take care of myself – how to stand on my own two feet. And as a I have gracefully aged, you have taught me – how to live. I can only hope that I have grown to be the woman that you are proud of. As I am a reflection of God and you.

A special thanks to my sister (April), my brother (Matthew), and my friend (LaShayla) who have supported me. Thank you for listening with such open ears and loving hearts as I have discussed my daily adventures, read my latest stories, or recited my favorite pieces of poetry/prose over the phone. Thank you for allowing me to bounce ideas off of you guys during our family's Thanksgiving and Christmas dinners. Thank you for truly believing that my work is just as great as anyone else who has ever written a book and been successful.

A special thanks to my husband (Curtis) who has loved me. Thank you for encouraging me to expand my writing platform. I would not ever dreamed of creating a blog or joining a variety of social media sites if it had not been for you. These platforms have motivated me to write consistently and allowed me to connect with so many genuine people from all over the world. Also, thank you for your attempts to make sense of poetry/prose, although I know there were many times you would rather have read a Fantasy or Science Fiction novel (smile). By the way, I love you and look forward to us growing stronger together.

A special thanks to my father (Bernard) as well as each and every loving family member, beautiful friend, passionate dental team member, positive mentor, loyal patient, faithful blog (*The Ninth Life*) follower, devoted social media follower, and dedicated reader ... thank you for *touching* and *changing* my life.

With Love, Dr. K. L.

From The Author's Desk

Thank you so much for reading *Every Day Isn't Perfect, Volume I: Change Begins With You First*. I appreciate you taking time out of your schedule to read it. If you enjoyed it, please leave a review.

Other Titles Written By The Author

Every Day Isn't Perfect, Volume II: Joy Comes In The Morning

Connect With Me On Social Media:

Twitter: @ iamklregister

Facebook: facebook.com/iamklregister

Linked In: Dr. K. L. Register

Blog: The Ninth Life

Made in the USA
San Bernardino, CA
14 May 2018